The Gentle Ravings of an Egomaniacal Master

M. L. Cerpok

PublishAmerica
Baltimore

First printing

At the specific preference of the author, PublishAmerica allowed this work to remain exactly as the author intended, verbatim, without editorial input.

ISBN: 1-4241-3834-5
PUBLISHED BY PUBLISHAMERICA, LLLP
www.publishamerica.com
Baltimore

Printed in the United States of America

I would like to dedicate this book to my students;
when in doubt, you have reassured me,
when attacked, you have defended me,
when in pain, you have healed me,
when alone, you have kept company with me.

Without you, I am a man, eccentric and without vocation. Because of you I am a teacher, and there is no greater gift which I could receive.

And-

To my children, who often sacrificed my presence in their lives so that I could be present in the lives of those in need.

Koan

Between some chapters, you will notice that there are short riddles. These are designed to assist the reader in finding a new or different perspective. They can be very frustrating to solve, but one hint: do not always assume that words should be taken literally. The Koan within this text are original and unique to Byakko Ryu Jujutsu.

Good Luck!

Contents

PREFACE

Why, you might ask, should I write a book? Well, for the same reason Bob Dylan sang songs. It's not like I can do it well, or that people even need to hear what I have to say. But there is only so much room in my head these days, and I felt that it was about time to clear out some of the rubbish. And like the esteemed Mr. Dylan, there will no doubt be some who say that this trash would have been better left to rot in my brain, yet there will be others who read the very same words and become inspired to make great changes in their lives. I write this book for both groups equally.

I also decided to write this book because, quite frankly, I can't seem to remember where I put my left, black sock yesterday. It was a brand new sock, only worn a half a dozen times, yet I had become somewhat fond of the way it fit. Now, with only one of the pair left, I feel that I have missed my opportunity for complete comfort on at least one day each week. This event has caused me to go into deep introspection, where many events in my life have likewise caused me to go, and from that introspection came the frightful notion that perhaps, just possibly, there will come a day when I am no longer able to adequately regurgitate to the masses the many incredibly deep and profound thoughts that I have had over the years.

So, I decided to go through the vault of my mind, and dig up what I could find. (Hey, now there's a sentence that even Bob Dylan could use.) What I found were a few chapters worth of stuff that seemed like a good idea to me at some time in my life and with a little editing, and some revision taking into account the effect that Jose Cuervo has had on me over the years, I have put it all down for you here in this text. But I feel that I must give an accounting of myself before we jump in with both boots on. The following information is necessary for you to fully understand the reasons for my self-centeredness.

I was born a poor black child…no, no…that's the beginning of a Steve Martin film.

I had, from an early age, reason to believe that I was special. You see, when I was in the first grade a gentleman named Arthur Shay decided to write a book on human reproduction called How a Family Grows. He chose our family as the showpiece of his story because my mother was pregnant, and there were already five children in our home. My mother was also the president of the PTA, complete with mini-skirt and go-go boots (it was the sixties). She was vivacious and outspoken, and the only thing that could have made the picture more complete was if we lived in Harper Valley.

But we didn't. We lived right on the border between the suburbs of Evanston and Skokie, Illinois, just outside of Chicago. Well, my brother, sisters, and I became instant celebrities in our schools as we had a photographer following us around and taking pictures for the book. In fact, I remember having my first celebrity fit when they decided that they needed one more picture to make the book complete, but I had already been told that we were finished. In true pop icon fashion, I refused to enjoy the experience of being famous and pouted through that entire photo session. Being, already at six years old, a true believer in sticking to one's ethics I made sure that they were as miserable as I. To this day I have a copy of that book on my mantel, with a first page picture of me looking glum amongst my smiling brothers and sisters.

My father was raised in a Jewish home, while my mother was raised Catholic. As a result, by the time I was thirteen I had studied both

Judaism in Hebrew School and Christianity in Sunday school and arrived as a freshman in high school with more questions than answers about my spirituality. My father, who was searching for his own answers to a seemingly miraculous recovery from a terrible bout with cancer, had been bringing home books about spiritualism and religion and I threw myself into a study of all of them. Hinduism, Buddhism, Islam, and books written by New Age authors all held a certain promise, but in the end I was still not convinced that any ONE of them had the answers that I felt I needed.

After reading a series of books by Carlos Castaneda, wherein he found his spiritual identity with the help of hallucinogenic substances, I began a three year adventure into the world of LSD and whatever else I thought might bring me to a greater understanding of why things are the way they are. This study brought me into the realm of such great thinkers and philosophers as Pink Floyd, the Doors, and of course Bob Dylan. Ah, the answer seemed so clear!

So, I joined a rock n' roll band and began writing. Lyrics were my forte, as I couldn't play an instrument, and so they made me the lead singer even though I couldn't sing (thank you Bob). Our band achieved some notoriety in our high school, at least to the point where several girls would follow us around campus and we were invited to cool parties. Knowing that I was now on the right path, I left high school prior to graduation and headed off to Hollywood, California to become the star I was destined to be. Needless to say, things did not work out as I planned in Hollywood (they rarely do) and so I made my way up the West Coast to Northern California, where I settled for a time in the Bay Area of San Francisco. It was *there* that I found my true path, and it was there that I started my career.

I arrived in the Bay Area in the very early 1980's and, shortly afterwards, I experienced several life-changing events. While driving back to California from a visit to Chicago, I was blessed with a personal *awakening*. This *awakening* occurred while driving through New Mexico and, while I may chronicle the event in detail at some later time, it remains the single most profound moment of my life. Suffice to say that, in that moment, the world stopped moving around me and I became aware of every fiber of my being. Now, it was also at that time that I became a parent. A somewhat simple task, for the father, compared to that of parenting itself. And, I began a study of Kung Fu under Mr. Scott Yoshida, which turned out not to be such a simple task.

Now, I wish I could say that my Kung Fu training was the stuff that movies are made of, that I stood for hours in stationary stances and was forced to repeat strikes and kicks thousands of times before being given an ounce of water, but in reality it only felt that way. The training was traditional, harsh at times and definitely the most physically difficult moments of my life. But I stuck with it and I was later offered the opportunity to become an instructor for the school.

This first experience in martial arts was an extremely insightful experience as I found that the martial arts, in its traditional sense, allowed for an effective spiritual search in the guise of an easily identifiable physical one. The total and complete attention to a single physical movement allowed for me to experience the empty mindedness that other attempts at meditation did not. I found that the philosophical knowledge that I had accumulated over the past seven years were indeed valuable if only I could rid myself of the clutter of thought that kept me from seeing the answers, which each path made available.

In 1986, I continued my journey up the west coast and landed in the sleepy little town of Olympia, Washington. I studied Tae Kwon Do under Grand Master Young Hak Lee for about three years, but as this was more of a sport style of martial arts, I realized that I had left the path of spiritual pursuit that made the pain and sacrifice of studying martial arts bearable. I left Lee's school and started to study Jujutsu under Professor Ron Jennings. While I saw the obvious practical self-defense application of Jujutsu (much more so than Kung Fu and Tae Kwon Do), I still missed the spiritual application. So, I opened a small training hall (called ChiDoKai Dojo) in my basement and began to offer instruction in the techniques of Kung Fu and Jujutsu as well as incorporating philosophy classes based upon my personal studies in Eastern and Western thought. Then another important event occurred.

During a seminar at my dojo, Professor Sig Kufferath (an extremely high ranking master of Jujutsu), complimented the physical and philosophical abilities of my students. He told me that he rarely saw, any longer, the etiquette and attention to character building that was apparent at my school. This was a man who traveled the world teaching martial arts, telling me that my students were on a path that was both healthy and wise. It was due, in part, to this conversation that shortly afterwards I separated from Professor Jennings in order to put my complete attention into developing a system of martial arts that would offer to students an alternative to sport martial arts, and a return to the traditional development of body, mind and spirit that had been the focus of martial arts for hundreds of years, but was no longer readily available to the public.

As more and more people became interested in my teachings, it became apparent that the myriad of movements and techniques I had drawn from my different martial arts experiences had begun to take on a form of its own. With the help of some of my more advanced students I began to catalog the variations of techniques I was teaching, as well as the new techniques and drills I was creating. This system has come to be known as Byakko Ryu Jujutsu and incorporates *The Study of True Understanding,* my personal philosophy of living well.

By the mid 1990's, ChiDoKai Dojo was home to more than a hundred students of the Byakko Ryu and had long since moved out of my basement. My student body was comprised of every type of person. At-risk children, individuals with handicaps, over-achievers, long time practitioners of the martial arts, police officers, and military Special Forces, all felt that this new system of training was both unique and practical.

Of course, Byakko Ryu Jujutsu and the thousands of students who have studied the system remain the focus of my life. This book started out as a way to share with those students some of the life skills that I felt would assist them in their quest for a more effective and satisfying way of living. But as I went further along in the process of the writing, I realized that the same lessons and stories that I use to convey a certain understanding in the concepts of a martial experience can be used by the average person to gain a greater awareness and appreciation for all aspects of daily life. I hope that you are one of those people, and that this book will bring you a truer understanding of the simplicity and joy that is available to everyone, every day.

On a final note, my wife has informed me that there are no left and right socks. Being that I have never once been wrong about something, I have investigated further. It appears that perhaps she is correct, in which case I have been living a lie in my ability to dress myself. Traveling further down this dangerous path of self doubt, I have conceived the notion that maybe, just maybe, I have been wrong about other things as well! Therefore, I must warn that if you should choose to continue reading this book, you may first want to go into your bedroom, open your sock drawer (I wonder if *everyone* has a sock drawer), and take a look for yourself. If indeed I am wrong about left and right socks, it may be that I am wrong about everything else, and all that is written on the pages that follow could be one big mistake.

And in the Beginning...

A bird sings in the far distance, faint but discernable. We stare, with breath held, into a dark well. The surface of the water is calm. It is deep, but very still. An overall sense of well being surrounds us. Suddenly, seemingly from out of nowhere, a huge brick is hurled into the well and the water erupts, splashing and spilling in all directions!

Ah, we are born.

Like the still water before the brick is dropped, we have a calm perspective of life prior to birth. But suddenly everything changes. There is light, there is cold, there is noise, there are faces. Good lord, the faces! There is a new perspective.

Soon, experiences of all types and fashion begin to shape who we are and who we will become. Some experiences we deem as good. Others we deem not so good, but as we near adulthood most all of us are fairly well lost.

A great number of the pages ahead will require the reader to try to see things through a different perspective. And like a well whose surface has become cluttered with leaves, twigs, and other debris, it will be necessary to remove some of the garbage before you can return to the calm stillness, which allows for new information to be seen with an open mind. Thus, the brick now comes!

In order to remove the layers of misunderstanding we must first and foremost be willing to admit that maybe we are WRONG about some things. Even if in the end it turns out that we did have a correct understanding, and arrive at a place of true understanding, we must be willing to put our ego aside and take a fresh approach. Is life simple for you? Is it effortless? If not, then there is most likely something that you misunderstand, something that you are approaching from a negative direction or possibly from a position of weakness.

I was speaking to a teen-aged student one day about some problems that she was experiencing at home. It was pretty typical stuff between a teen and her mother, for the most part. But the situation had deteriorated to the point where the two were barely speaking to one another. During the course of our conversation, I had the opportunity to ask her if she would like for me to give her some advice - changes she could easily make, to help create a more hospitable living environment. She said, quite frankly, "No!"

I asked her why not, and she replied that she could guess at the things that I would suggest and that she herself had already figured these things out. But, she went on, she felt that she was right in her expectations and that her mother was wrong; so why should she make concessions? I asked her if being right was more important than being effectively able to remedy the problems at home. She thought about this for a while. and then asked to be able to think about it a bit longer.

Unfortunately, most people would agree with this student. That *to be right is more important than to be effective*. I find it in politics. I find it in religion. I find it in some of the most obvious, and some of the most obscure, places. But in most cases, there it is. No matter how aware we become that this is indeed the case, we hold on to being right anyway!

So, what is this fascination we have with being right? Why would otherwise intelligent people choose to suffer through a situation, rather than admitting that maybe they are wrong? Is it the competition? Is it the status and recognition that we receive for being right? Ask yourself, if a major complication or roadblock in your life could be fixed by simply admitting that you are wrong, would you do it? I will bet you that if you are having difficulty in your life right now, there is something that you are not addressing correctly but you would insist that you are right! Why would I make this bet? Because life is effortless! If you are making "right" choices then life would seem simple and natural because *life is movement, in the most fundamental way*, towards a resolution of some kind.

I was fishing one time with my father and my grandfather on Perrualt Lake in Ontario, Canada. We had heard about another, smaller lake called Lost Lake where the big fish were. We asked a friend of ours, who was a guide on Perrualt Lake, to take us to the big fish in Lost Lake. He smiled at us, and said that there were no fish in Lost Lake. Well, we had heard this from him before about other fishing spots, and knew that we were right about Lost Lake. We eventually talked him into letting us hire him to take us out there. Much to our surprise, he pulled the boat up to an island in Perrualt Lake. He got out and started to pull the boat up onto the shore, so we all got out and helped him. He then instructed us to pick up the boat and carry it! Well, we did, and after some forty minutes of carrying this boat through the woods, we came to a small lake in the middle of the island. Lost Lake! We put the boat back in the water and began to fish. Three hours later we had not caught one fish! Then we had to pick up that stupid boat and carry it all the way back out to the main lake.

Two lessons I learned from this. One, we are not always right, no matter how sure we are. Two, it is much more effective to move a boat on water than it is on land! But so often we go through our lives like we are carrying our boat on land, stubbornly resisting that maybe, just maybe, we are wrong and should put the boat back in the water.

Try to remember that *perfection is an ever-changing state of being*. What was effective today may not be effective tomorrow. Be deeply rooted as the oak, yet on the surface, gently yielding as the reed. From this position of power, read on!

No stone will ever weigh as heavy,
as those which have yet to be formed.

The Oak

I vaguely remember when I was very young, first learning how to climb the stairs in our home. It wasn't easy. So, like all toddlers just learning to go up and down the stairs, I was very careful and climbed them slowly one step at a time. It wasn't long before I was experienced enough to lose my fear, and be much more confident in my ability to climb them.

I would look at those stairs and think, "I bet I could take those stairs two steps at a time." And so I tried it.

"No problem," I thought. Then one day I looked at those stairs, now so familiar and unimposing, and I thought, "You know, I'll bet I could take those stairs three steps at a time!" I started up then and there, without another thought, three steps at a time. I went right up, well.half way, anyway. Suddenly I missed a step, smacked my forehead on the stair above and slid unceremoniously to the bottom of the stairway. There I was, lying on the floor with a big bump (and a little blood) on my head and wondering what had hit me.

What had hit me was my first, though certainly not the last, lesson in the importance of a good foundation. You see, I could have taken those stairs three steps at a time if I had waited patiently to gain the experience and ability. But like many of the people whom I meet these days, I wanted to get to the top as fast as possible. I jumped right into an endeavor that was beyond my current abilities, too impatient to develop the necessary training and conditioning.

I would venture to guess that many of you did not start reading this book at the Preface, but rather you opened to a chapter somewhere in the middle, to a subject that you thought might be more interesting or fun and started there. Then you returned to the beginning after you had satisfied that urge for some immediate gratification. Welcome to the world of martial artists! If I had a dime for every student who wanted to learn the "secrets" of self defense within the first month of training. what, you don't know why I am talking about martial arts? Well, go back and read the preface!

One day in 1992, while I was putting the finishing touches on a new space for my expanding school, one of the construction workers asked about the success of my dojo.

"I have a friend," he told me, "who is an excellent martial artist. He wins a lot of tournaments. He sunk about thirty thousand dollars into opening up a school, but he had to close down about a year later and return to his previous job. You must have had quite a bit of money to put together a place this nice!"

I explained to him that I had actually started my first dojo without any capital at all. I had put together an abduction prevention lesson for my daughter, who was seven years old at the time. She enjoyed it so much that I decided to teach it through a local community center. After that, I taught the class for free at her elementary school. The children at her school gained so much from the lessons that some of their parents asked if I would teach martial arts to their children. I began teaching several students informally in my basement on a four foot by eight foot mat that I had borrowed from a friend. I began by teaching two children, then four, then eight children, and then two adults joined in the classes. Information about the classes I was teaching, as well as an appreciation for my teaching style, spread by word of mouth through our community. About a year later I was able to open a small commercial space outside of my home with forty students and a thousand dollars that I borrowed from my grandfather. It was only then that I decided to put some money into a small advertisement in the local yellow pages.

I try to teach my students that one sure secret of success is to not assume that you can put on the uniform of your teacher and know the art. Similarly, you should not start out with thousands of dollars of overhead and expect to succeed simply because you have a beautiful store front!

We are taught early in our study of the martial arts that all of the best and most effective techniques start with a proper stance. We are taught that only through patient understanding of how to stand up can we eventually learn to walk, and then to run and then to fly. Develop your stance, know your base first, then you can build your understanding sufficient to be successful at any endeavor.

One of your first steps in understanding how to defend yourself from an attacker is to learn to move from one place, or stance, to another. Your defense, your actions, will be inefficient and possibly ineffective if you attempt to move too soon or if you move too late. The same can be said in business negotiations, or even parenting. The ability to move at exactly the right moment is very important, and it can only be developed by first learning how to stand in one place with balance and poise. Then we can learn how to move from that stationary stance to another stance and place with careful deliberation. After much training and practice in moving from one stance to another, you develop the ability to move as needed, without forethought or deliberation. Only then can you begin learning and practicing movement from any one place to any other place with smoothness, certainty, and spontaneous agility.

When I left home at the age of eighteen, I thought I knew pretty much all there was to know about life and the world. I was certain that I would go out and make my mark! Imagine how surprised I was to find myself working at a fast food joint just a short time later, and living off of Malt O' Meal and turkey pot pies that I could buy one day after expiration for thirteen cents each. After several months I managed to find work at a martial arts supply store (an interesting coincidence) turned tourist trap on Hollywood Boulevard. That was where I learned my first lessons in business.

The owner of the store was an older man who also owned stores in two other locations. He started me out stocking shelves and then slowly and carefully taught me the retail business. I worked from eight o'clock in the morning until two o'clock the next morning, and then walked ten blocks home to get four and a half hours of sleep before getting up and doing it again. I did this every day except Sundays, when my hours were ten o'clock in the morning until midnight. One year was all it took until I knew how to run a retail shop with my eyes closed, literally.

Two years later, when I first began my study of Kung-Fu, I remembered those long days as I stood for what seemed like an eternity in a Horse Stance. If you ever have to stand in a Horse Stance you'll know that fifteen minutes can seem like an eternity! But it was nothing compared to what that old merchant had demanded of a young kid who'd come in off the street looking for a job.

After I left Southern California, I never again had trouble finding work. I had developed an incredible work ethic, and had gained a valuable skill in retail management. I held management positions at two stores simultaneously several years later, and both stores did fantastically well. It all resulted from a good foundation.

Unfortunately, few of us possess the wisdom to recognize the value of a solid foundation when we start on a new endeavor. We are too busy looking ahead, at where we want and expect to be, to pay attention to the trivial, boring stuff that lies at the beginning of our path. Yet our very success lies in our foundations, in that same trivial, boring stuff, rather than in our anticipations or imagined expectations!

Anticipatory Expectations

You know, if you hadn't expected for the last chapter to hold some deep insight, you wouldn't be feeling so disappointed! But really…

One of my younger students left the dojo after class one day while I was fishing in the parking lot out front (I was on vacation that week). He sat in his car for a little while speaking with his mother. Then they got out and came back up to talk to me. She said that he had a little problem, and maybe I could help him. I asked what the problem was.

She said, "Well he wants to know…he thinks that he should be getting a promotion in rank, but he was just told that he's not supposed to ask for promotions. So we're wondering, you know, how does he get his promotion if he's not supposed to ask?"

I asked the boy, "Do you see what I'm doing?"

He said, "Yeah, you're fishing."

I said, "Yep, I'm fishing in the parking lot. Do you think I'm going to catch anything?"

He said, "No."

I asked, "Do you think there's any chance at all that I'm going to catch anything?"

Again, he said, "No."

"So," I pressed, "why do you think that I'm fishing?"

He thought about it for a second, and then he said, "Because you like it?"

"That's right, I enjoy fishing." Then I continued, "Do you come to Jujutsu to catch promotions?"

"No," he laughed.

"Well, why do you come?"

"To learn stuff."

"Why? Why do you come here to learn stuff? You want to catch promotions?"

"No," he laughed again, "because I have fun!"

I said, "Oh, so you enjoy doing Jujutsu. Listen, I'm going to be on vacation for the rest of the week, do you think you're going to get your promotion this week?"

"No," he rightly replied.

"Should you still come to Jujutsu?" I asked.

"Yeah."

"Why?"

"Cause I like it."

"Then don't worry about your promotion. Focus on the enjoyment of what you are doing, and the rewards will seem to come quickly. But, *when you're doing something simply for the reward, the reward will seem to take a long time in coming.*"

The anticipation of expected results keeps us from focusing on the enjoyment of our endeavors. This does not mean that we should not have goals. But, once set, the goals must not remain the focus of our daily activities, lest we find that years of anticipation have cost us the pleasure of experiencing day-to-day events.

On a similar note, many times I have been asked the question, "Why do bad things happen to good people?" This can be a very difficult question to answer, not because of its surface complexity, but because the individual asking the question has already put a value judgment (good or bad) on the situation. I would have to ask them, "What *bad* thing are you referring to?" and "What led you to see these things as *bad*?"

Most often I find that people view outcomes as negative because of an anticipated, or expected, result. If we are able to remove anticipation and expectation from our endeavors and our relationships, we will find a wonderful surprise awaits us each day. As events unfold we are neither disappointed nor are we gratified. Each day we wake up (if we wake up) and say, “Ah, I am alive, the world as we knew it last night exists and today is as today should be!” And if somehow throughout the day we find that the world, or our place within it, has changed we can say, “Ah, the world is different for me today, and it is as it should be!”

Here is where many may take me wrong. I am not saying to be complacent, lazy, or idle. Commitment to action is what is called for! Live each day to the fullest of your ability, but don’t do it in anticipation of an expected reward. Plan for, but don’t expect, the end result. It hasn’t happened yet. Living in the past is an anchor, and living in the future is an illusion! Living in the moment that is right now is effective.

I remember growing up in Chicago, watching professional ice hockey. Our team would be down by a goal (or more) and the team would be passing the puck around looking for just the right opening for the shot. The fans would yell, “Shoot, Shoot, SHOOT!” Seize the moment, take the opportunity! SHOOT THE PUCK! And sometimes the team would shoot, and score a goal. Sometimes they would shoot, and not score a goal. But, Bret Hull (one of the greatest hockey players to ever play the game) once said when asked how he was able to score so many times, “I just shoot the puck at the net and sometimes it goes in.” What a simple thought. *Take the shot. Sometimes it goes in.*

However, I must interject that another reason for judging a situation as bad is that we have missed the opportunity for growth, which always accompanies hardship in our lives. I had an adult student who, through our discussions, made it very clear that he had issues with death. He had experienced the untimely death of a friend during childhood and felt that this person had given up on life. His view of death was shaped at that time and he vowed he would never let death take him so easily! During the course of our relationship, a very dear friend of ours was diagnosed with an inoperable brain tumor and six months to live. When our friend came to me for spiritual guidance, I advised him to take each day as it came as they were still exploring treatments, to keep a positive attitude as miracles do happen, but also to put his affairs (physical and spiritual) in order so as to be ready and able to transition easily into the next stage of his existence. My student was appalled! He felt that I should not have said anything to this young man other than "Fight!"

As of this writing, it remains to be seen whether or not my student learned anything this second time around. We can only hope that he did, as death is a natural part of life and he will, most likely, have to experience it many more times before his time comes.

But whether we see things as "good" and "bad" due to our expectations of a desired result or because of the given opportunity for our growth, those answers do not address why these things happened to someone else, or what the catalyst was for things happening to us. However, the answer to this can be easily explained by the concept of *karma*. Both the Old and New Testaments of the bible teach us that there will be "an eye for an eye," that "as ye sow, so shall ye reap," and to "judge not, lest ye be judged." Of course, many Eastern philosophies state very plainly that we must live many life times in order to make right our wrongs and give our selves the opportunity for spiritual growth.

I do not mind if people shy away from the concept of karma, as it is such a prevalent theme in most all of religious thought, that I realize they are intimidated or uncomfortable by the word rather than the idea. Often people confuse the idea of karma with that of reincarnation, which may be completely unacceptable within their belief system. But, I have always been able to help comfort people going through hardship with the notion that they, or someone that they know, is simply "balancing the books" and this is necessary in order for us to mature, spiritually.

I tell my young students about the concept of karma in order to get them to think before they speak or act. As some are developing the rebelliousness that is natural in young people, it is difficult to convince them to act in accordance with our rules due to a threat of consequences imposed by a figure of authority, whether that is a parent, the police, or even God. But they do respond quite well to the idea that every cruel act, every mean word, will come back to them. That to live an effortless life requires a "balanced book" and that they are accumulating liability or assets even now.

Live your life according to the ethics that you have developed, and that you are developing, through the moments of your life. Look for the good that you can do without expectation of reward, and err on the side of giving too much. Do not be afraid to "fail" at your endeavors because the attempt is always an opportunity for growth. You will be or you will not be with us tomorrow and therefore, either way, you must seize today!

The moon rises in the East.
The forest trees rain up to the sky
intercepting its path.
The moon sets in the West.

Cease the Struggle

"Kaihoo suru" (complete release) is what I teach my students to strive for, and attain. I want them to achieve complete and total freedom so that they can live a life that satisfies them. I call this living effortlessly, and we discuss it often in our classes.

The question has been raised that what I am advocating seems to be the opposite of what people hear elsewhere. So many philosophies and religions seem certain that life is a struggle, that much of the value in life is only achievable through struggle. I've been asked why I say that we should be living effortlessly. Shouldn't we be struggling, working hard in life?

Attainment of effortless living is your goal, but it is far from effortless to attain. You have effortless living when you're born, but we lose that as we age. The struggle in life is trying to regain that effortless living, and to maintain it.

Professor Kano, the founder of Judo, was known to call for "minimum effort, maximum effect" in the performance of technique. I am simply talking about taking that concept into your life. I'm not saying effortless in the sense of doing nothing, but rather to learn to expend your effort efficiently, for maximum results. Don't spin your wheels without effect.

Effortless living is accepting the moment and dealing with it appropriately. It is elimination of second thoughts brought on by worries and doubts, and having the ability to act as needed in each moment.

Struggle is very important, it is a part of the way our lives work, a part of nature. But, we don't start out that way. When we're born, we're not struggling. We get a swat on the behind, we take a breath and life is good. Even if we are abused or neglected, we don't really know enough to judge the quality of our life, we only know that we're alive, which is good. So we start out living effortlessly, all we know is to live.

Then, as we grow up, we interact with others and we learn to struggle through life. We learn to make our lives better, to want to improve our lives, to strive for a situation that we like more. We learn that we should struggle, so we do. Unfortunately, most people struggle for the rest of their lives. They struggle right up until the day they die. Even into the moment of dying, some will continue to struggle.

The point of what we're doing, in trying to develop an effortless life, is ceasing the struggle. Interestingly, the characters which make up the word "karate," which many people think of as a fighting term, can be interpreted as "ceasing the struggle." This can be extremely difficult.

Consequently, even if we were suddenly aware at an early age of what to do and how to do so, it will still require quite a bit of struggle, and getting through a lot of adversity, to get to the point of living effortlessly. For one thing, people won't like you very much. You start to live an effortless life, and I guarantee that one of the first things you'll notice, as you become more successful at living effortlessly, is that people don't like it. Most people don't like to see other people not struggling. They think that there's something wrong with you, or you're not playing the game right. They may also think that you're arrogant. They may think that you think you're superior to everyone else. Actually you're just living effortlessly and they're struggling, and there's a huge contrast between the two.

Even while you are first learning to live effortlessly, you will find people who will resent your attempt. Family, friends, and co-workers may actually begin to feel worse about their situation in contrast to the improvements that you're making in your life, and they may hold you responsible for their own perception of their lives getting worse.

Therefore, the path that you're taking, going from effortless living back to effortless living, is a struggle in many ways. But, it doesn't have to take the rest of your life. You can do it in a very short time. If you stay focused and disciplined, it could be done in three years. If you do it by reading many books, attending different churches or studying one "way" after another, then it could take as long as twenty years. Either path may end in the same place, and is perfectly valid. After all, *there are many veins upon the leaf, but all paths lead to the outer edge*. But why bother taking the longer route, to prolong the struggle for effortless living? We should take the efficient path, as effectively as possible getting to the point where we can live effortlessly.

Life is good. When I wake up in the morning, I often say, "What a beautiful morning!" Not because the sky is clear, but because I woke up. Any morning you wake up is going to be a beautiful day. You're alive. You've just been granted another opportunity to experience all the joy and mystery and adventure of life. You should love living.

This reminds me of a short story, which I previously had published, called The Big Bag of Rocks. It is the story of a man who started out life full of the wonder of all things. But as he went through his life he began collecting rocks, negative events, which he carried in a bag across his shoulder. Needless to say, as life went on, the man was weighed down and miserable by the accumulative weight of the bag of rocks. His previously wonderful existence seemed to have suddenly turned difficult and effortful.

Living becomes effortless when we are living fully in the moment with true understanding of ourselves, and our place in the world. We are holding our heads high, witnessing the wonder of the nature of all things. Living is effortless because we are no longer beset by worries, doubts, and fears. We have left our bag of rocks behind. We know what to do, because we understand what is important in our lives and we have learned the nature of our passions. We are not anchored to memories and second thoughts about what has happened, nor do we spend our time and energy worrying about what might happen in the future. We have learned to live effectively right now, even as we understand that what has been, and what could be, flow perfectly into and out of the moment we are now experiencing. We spend the moment as it is, within the event, learning and knowing. Then we proceed onward to the next moment, leaving the rocks behind. It is the natural, and effortless, order of things.

Do not confuse hard work with living with effort. Effortless living is not easy, nor is it lazy. Living effortlessly will often require a great deal of hard work, but the work is effortless in the sense that we now know what to do and how to act. We are not bowed over by the accumulated weight of a lifetime of trauma and emotional turmoil. Our hard work is performed at our will and to our purpose. We live, we love, we work, and our fatigue is borne with satisfaction because we understand that we have earned it meaningfully.

One could argue that ancient peoples lived effortlessly because they lived in the moment. Did I eat today? Did my family eat today? Did I get killed today by the elements? No, then life is good.

Modern life isn't quite so simple. We are surrounded, and bombarded every day by choices that we could make. We perceive so many opportunities for pleasure, so many things that we could have, so many places we could go. We're taught to believe that life is complex. Life has become a marketplace, with so many choices to make. It's as if we are a child wandering through a candy store with a handful of nickels and dimes. We're not really sure what we can not afford, nor can we make a decision on what we want because there's so much to choose from.

Don't be deluded into thinking that you must have it all, that your life will be incomplete without some new gadget or new experience. The satisfaction that we derive from such activity is often empty, and without lasting substance. We end up obsessed with seeking out something else, always grasping for something newer in the mistaken belief that then we will be satisfied.

Seek out affirmations of the joy and beauty of Life. Do not look out onto the world through glass all cracked and glazed over by the gray dust of fatigue and dissatisfaction. Music, poetry, prayer or a sunrise are all excellent means to regularly re-affirm the beauty of life. Listen to the Beatles' "Dear Prudence." There's a simple reminder of beauty and love.

I've used the Lord's Prayer as my affirmation for years, even though I'm not a Christian. But I love the prayer and the meanings within it. I mentally recite the Lord's Prayer when I meditate. I started using it, and I continue to do so, because I think that it is a perfect reminder of how we should be living our lives:

"Our Father who art in Heaven."

(This can be a reference to whatever we choose to believe in as the source of all being, even if it is something as formless in concept as the Tao.)

"Hallowed be thy name."

(This is an expression of awe and respect for that source of being.)

"Thy kingdom come, thy will be done, on Earth as it is in Heaven."

(Don't wait to die, and be in God's kingdom, before you start acting the way that you believe God wants you to act. If you think that God wants you to live a certain way, you should live that way now, here on Earth. Don't just go to church every Sunday, or say a certain amount of prayers, or bow to the East so many times a day. Don't just follow the basic rules to get into God's good graces so that you can go to Heaven and then say, "Okay, now I'll stop doing all those bad things I was doing." Too few people actually fully live their beliefs. Most just live well enough to think that they are going to heaven. Just good enough, by their judgment, that they'll get to where they think they want to go.)

"Give us this day our daily Bread."

(Allow us the opportunity and physical strength to earn a living and to feed and care for our families.)

"Forgive us our trespasses as we forgive those who trespass against us."

(We must learn acceptance. We must be able to forgive others for the errors that we, ourselves, are going to make.)

"Lead us not into temptation but deliver us from evil."

(Help us to see and understand the difference between growth and stagnation. Give us the fortitude to make the difficult choices when it comes to things that we know aren't the "right" thing to do, but sure are tempting. We need strength when we face those decisions.)

"For yours are the Power and the Glory."

(This is a second acknowledgment of our belief in this source of all being.)

I like to say, "*Do your bit for God and God will do his bit for you.*" The Lord's Prayer is applicable to most spiritual beliefs, and it is always my reminder of how to live well.

We all need some kind of regular affirmation that life is good. Many of us spend too much of our lives convinced that life is bad, that it's unfair and a constant struggle. We believe that life is uncertain, that it's one problem after another, one bill after another, one disappointment after another, one failure after another. We become programmed to see, pick out, and remember all the negatives in life.

When we start to see and recognize the beauty in the world, the next step is to see and understand that we are a part of that beauty. When we've convinced ourselves of the beauty of the world, and we understand that we are a part of it all, we will begin to understand that we, too, are beautiful. We are potentially as beautiful as everything around us.

Fishing in the Parking Lot

For many years, while developing my first *dojo*, or training hall, I would refrain from taking time off from my teaching for vacations. There were two main reasons for this. First, I truly enjoyed my work and so where was I to go, that would bring me a greater pleasure? Second, when developing any type of business it is very important to the success of the business that the owner should be there! But after several years had gone by, some of my students insisted that I should take some time off. So, each year I would spend my "Summer Vacation" sitting in a chair out in front of the dojo. I spent some of that time, on a warm summer afternoon, discussing my philosophy of living effectively with one of my students:

I sat down in front of the dojo this morning. I'm on vacation, you know, and I was thinking I haven't gone fishing in quite a long time. I keep my fishing pole here at the dojo, so I got it out and started cleaning it up. Then I thought, since my fishing pole is nice and clean, I may as well do a little fishing. So I started fishing, sitting in a chair outside the dojo, casting into the parking lot. I was amused by the reactions of people. Everybody that came up to me would say, "What are you doing?"

So, I would laugh and say, "I'm fishing. What does it look like I'm doing?"

One of them responded, "You should be fishing in the water."

And I said, "No, if I go in the water then I'll scare the fish away."

"No, no," he said, "why are you fishing in the parking lot? Why aren't you at the lake or something?"

And so I answered him, "Well, I love being here at the dojo. I run into many of my friends here at the dojo, yes? And the fish aren't biting anyway. My goodness, it's 3:00 in the afternoon and 90 degrees out, there's not a cloud in the sky. It's not like I'm going to catch anything anyway! So, I may as well sit and talk to my friends. Isn't that why I go fishing anyway? That's why I used to go fishing with my father, to sit in the boat and talk to him."

But what I find most interesting is that everybody is asking me what I'm doing, when it's quite obvious what I'm doing. I'm fishing. But what they don't realize is that all I'm really doing is what I try to do every moment of every day: living and enjoying it. All of the time, whether I'm spending my vacation in a chair outside my school, or doing something else that seems silly to others. This is true even at times that aren't so silly, such as if I'm angry or sad about something. I can be angry with a situation without losing my joy for living. Whatever emotion there is - anger, sadness, happiness - you should live life in such a way as to be able to find joy and satisfaction with what it is that you're doing, every minute of every day of your life. Sometimes, fishing in the parking lot is a good reminder. At least to me, it's a good reminder that no matter what you're doing, or how you *feel* about what you're doing, you have to enjoy it. You have to enjoy every moment.

Now I must ask you, the reader, if you died today would you be satisfied with how you spent yesterday? And if you died tomorrow, would you be satisfied with how you spent today? Most people answer no. If they had known that they had only one day left to live they would have done something differently.

Well, do you know that you're not going to die tomorrow? No, nobody knows that. So, what if you assumed that today is the last day, because tomorrow hasn't come yet and you really don't know what will happen? Wouldn't you want to enjoy more completely what you're doing today?

But some people would argue, "Well if you're going to look at it that way, why not just quit your job and go fishing?" And I'd have to say, that sounds like a marvelous idea if that is what will truly bring you satisfaction today. But what they may not realize is that quitting their job and going fishing isn't necessarily satisfying. What if their focus in such an endeavor is to catch fish? What if the fish do not want to be caught that day? Now you have spent the rest of your life sitting miserably in a boat.

We all have certain responsibilities. We may need to earn a living, to support our family or what have you. There are things we should *choose* to do because we have those responsibilities or commitments to ourselves and others. However, we should still enjoy them. We should still enjoy and find satisfaction in what we're doing, regardless of what it is we're doing.

The point is not that you should quit your job and then seek out something that you enjoy doing, although that may be necessary for some people to do. Many people put themselves into jobs that don't fit them. The criteria that people use when choosing a job or career - pay, hours, and benefits - often have little or nothing to do with who they are, or what they love. They try to convince themselves that they shouldn't have to *be* their job. Well of course they don't want to be their job, they hate their job. And so they convince themselves that it's okay, because they'll just separate who they are from their work. They say, "I'm only at work eight hours a day, and then I come home and I have nothing to do with that until tomorrow."

But it simply isn't true. We come home, and we think about our day. We talk about what happened at work with our spouse or family. Concerns about work nag at us while we sleep; you know everybody dreams about their work some time. As a result, how many hours of the day are we really spending concentrating and focusing on something that we dislike rather than doing the same for something that we enjoy?

Many people, who believe that they can be detached from their work, simply are not. You can see it in their lives. They may not talk about their work. They may take long vacations from their work. But, invariably two things happen: number one, their work suffers and number two, they and their families suffer. It all comes out somewhere.

Think about it. You're not enjoying something that takes up at least half of your waking life. Consider the time spent from the minute you wake up in the morning until you get back in bed. Include commuting time, time spent discussing the day, and thoughts or worries as you're falling asleep. At least half of your adult life is spent not enjoying life, simply because you don't enjoy your work.

You know, when people realize the truth in what I say they may quit their jobs. Because when you put it that way, they find it hard to argue. It sounds even worse once you begin discussing their home life. I ask them, "Hey, you sound so unhappy, what's the deal?"

"Well, my wife," or "It's my husband…" and so on. By the time they're done talking about it, they realize that between work and home almost all of their waking life is spent being miserable.

But that really doesn't mean everyone should quit their job, or leave their husband or wife. What it means is that each of us must learn to find joy in each moment. Some individuals may truly need to quit a job or end a relationship, in order to realign themselves with what is important to them. But *running from your unhappiness will not lead you to happiness.* The point is that you should learn to enjoy what it is that you're doing, right now. You have to learn to enjoy the moment. Kind of like what I was doing while fishing in the parking lot.

I have often spoken to students about truth and being honest with other people. But along with being honest with others comes being honest with ourselves; to acknowledge and pursue the moments that will truly make us happy. The philosophy of The Study of True Understanding says that you should show concern and caring for other people and acceptance of their happiness. It does not say that the concerns and cares of others should dictate our personal actions. We must take time to find who we truly are. We need to figure out what truly satisfies us personally, while learning to distinguish satisfaction from pleasure. And also, to be honest with ourselves about what are our needs. To be able to look at ourselves and figure out what we are attached to, and what are our needs, this is an early awareness skill!

For example, how many people actually sit down and try to figure out their passion, what they really want to do with their life? A large percentage of people never really work it out. Another large percentage get stuck in jobs that they don't really want or appreciate because they chose to pursue something that seemed like a good idea, initially, rather than pursuing their own personal passions.

At one time I was employed as the general manger for the original Strip O Gram, a novelty telegram company that was big in the late 1970s and '80s. I traveled regularly to several cities where I'd spend a weekend interviewing and hiring dancers. I was twenty-five years old at the time, and you can probably imagine that it seemed like a wonderful job, just wonderful. Yes, it was exciting and fun for a while but it soon became tedious and boring, because it had very little to do with how I saw myself as a person. So I had to stop and take some time to figure out what was missing in my life.

One of the things I realized was that I was often hiring people who were in bad situations. Once hired, they were required to be healthy and drug free, so I found myself teaching people how to live well and helping them to find satisfaction for themselves. I thought to myself, well this is an odd way of helping people.

At that time I had been studying martial arts for several years, and I enjoyed assisting my teachers in the instruction of other students. I realized that it would be much more effective to help people in a context where they'll actually be asking to learn. It's much more efficient to help people who are ready for, and actively seeking, change in their lives. I was able to identify my passion, teaching people how to find satisfaction and happiness in their lives, and to then find an efficient and enjoyable way to exercise my passion. But there are far too many people out there who haven't even begun to take that first step yet.

I'll tell you a short story. Remember my friend, the fishing guide up at Perrualt Lake? One evening, when I was about fourteen years old, I was fishing with him off of the dock in front of the lodge. It was a beautiful Canadian sunset. I asked him about his "work" as a guide.

"Don't you ever get tired of work; taking people out in boats day after day and helping them catch fish?" His reply helped shape the rest of my life.

He told me that when he was a young child, his grandfather would take him out fishing every day. Their family hunted and fished for the majority of their food, and it was just something that you did, naturally. Every day, while fishing, they would sit and talk. His grandfather would share old stories, and words of wisdom. Sometimes they would just sit in silence. He told me that these were the fondest memories of his life. "I don't go to work at all," he told me, "I go fishing."

Decades later, when a friend asked me how I was able to put in so many hours at my martial arts school without ever seeming to lose my enthusiasm, I told him "All I do is go and play with my friends every day for hours on end. I have been doing that since I was a child. How does one lose their enthusiasm for playing with their friends?"

We must learn to replace the word *work*, in regard to our jobs, with the word *career*. In order to truly enjoy every moment of our day, we need to learn to alter our perspective of our *vocations*, so that we can see our careers as constant *vacations*.

Identify who you are. Identify your truths, your passions. Identify your falsehoods as well, particularly in relation to the people around you. We often incorporate many falsehoods into our lives simply because we feel they're necessary for the satisfaction of the other people in our lives. But are your falsehoods really helping others, or are you only encouraging their own falsehoods? How much of our personal relationships with others are supported by falsehoods, little white lies, minor omissions of the truth? Recognize that removing the lies from your own life will remove lies and falsehoods from other's lives as well.

Next, embrace the person that you are, learning to like who you are. Make sure you have accurately identified who you are and learn to like it. You will know that you have hit upon truth in identification when life suddenly becomes so much simpler and satisfyingly effective. Live that truth as every part of every day. Make it so that who you've discovered yourself to be and the *persona that you project* are actual representations of YOU. Then you will find that there are things you do in life because they are a part of who you are. There are other things in life that you do because you have come to believe that it is what is expected of you. Finally, and simply, begin to live your life according to who you really want to be, not based upon who others tell you to be.

I had an instructor who used to tease me saying, "You know, it's easy for you to say all this stuff because look at your life. You have the easiest life of anyone in the world." And I would laugh because she obviously didn't know me that well. I can't remember, for sure, the number of times that I've almost died. I've been homeless twice. But it just so happened that my experiences, along with my studies, caused me to become aware. So I tell students now, "Just do what I say, when I say, how I say and you'll be a happier person." I don't mind if that amuses them, because I know it's not that big of a chore.

There's no mystical secret to being happy, it's pretty easy. We're conditioned to assume that meaning in life must be esoteric. But life is simple, so keep it that way.

Now, don't confuse the messenger with the message, the container with the contents. I've discussed this many times with my students, as they tend to put much more emphasis on the person I am, instead of what I teach. They want to know what I eat, how I sleep. But I am simply the tool, a conduit for the understanding that I bring to others. I joke with people about my being right all the time. But in fact, it is truly humbling for me to watch people attempt the way that I tell them is a simpler way to live and to see their lives just completely change around.

During the course of my studies I have learned and practiced many healing techniques. One thing that I have learned from my experiences as a healer is that the healer isn't healing anyone. People are healing themselves. People, who strongly believe in my power to heal them, are more easily and effectively healed. What I do now is very much like healing. I'm not *making* my students become aware of the joy and satisfaction that can be found in every moment. I'm simply a catalyst, the motivator for them to see the joy for themselves. I use lessons in Byakko Ryu Jujutsu and the eight principles of The Study of True Understanding as tangible ways of showing my students how to begin the process of becoming aware, and how to enjoy the experience.

Four winds blow.
Birds will fly here and there.
A boat drifting down river cares not.

Disciplined Breathing

I sold my car in the spring of 1996 and bought a bicycle. I rode the bicycle, or walked just about every place that I went that summer. It was amazing to me how much beauty I'd been missing. We miss so much when we're driving our cars. We don't hear the birds singing. We don't hear the children playing. We don't feel the light breezes, though we may feel a stiff wind through the car window. We don't see the clouds. We don't really see trees because we're flying by at forty-five miles per hour, or faster.

When we're walking, we learn to appreciate so much more than when we're driving a car. We can appreciate more because we've slowed ourselves down. This is one reason why I recommend breathing exercises and meditation. It slows us down, and allows us to recognize just what a beautiful world we live in. Those moments of silence and inactivity also allow us to understand that we are a part of a beautiful world, and that we are beautiful as well. This understanding is essential if we are to find *True Understanding.*

It is really quite simple to learn to breathe with discipline, yet most people find it extremely difficult to practice. This is most likely because we are programmed to not have idle moments, after all, "Idle hands are the devil's workshop," they say. Hence, when you first start it is important to schedule your breathing exercise much in the same way you would schedule any other type of exercise. I began the practice of *sitting meditation* when I was in my teens, and exercised my breathing daily, for many years. When I was in my thirties I was able to meditate for as long as fifteen hours at a time. Further, I wholly attribute my personal awakening to the practice of disciplined breathing.

Start out with a deep cleansing breath. Then, inhale through your nose, allowing for your belly to expand. Breathing with your chest is ineffective, even if you look better doing it that way! Exhale through pursed lips, as if blowing through a straw. This will allow you to control the speed of your exhale. Breathe out for twice as long as you breathe in. A good starting point is to count to four as you inhale, and count to eight as you exhale. Eventually, you can work your count higher. I currently breathe one breath per minute (five seconds in, fifty-five seconds out) when I practice.

There are many benefits to disciplined breathing. For one, it is extremely relaxing and lowers our blood pressure. We also learn, through disciplined breathing, discipline of the body. This requires a discipline of the mind, which leads to effortless breathing and in turn leads to effortless thought because we see life unfold one moment at a time.

What we will begin to understand, as we are able to isolate and recognize one moment at a time, is that each moment holds the beauty of opportunity within it. Every moment holds a potentially beautiful experience. If we're not living with the awareness of each moment of our day we may, in fact, miss the beauty of the day. Breathing exercises slow us down, teaching us to focus on every breath and upon every second of each breath. When we learn to focus on those moments, we will begin to see and experience beauty in the moment. Our recognition that we are a part of all that beauty helps us believe that we deserve those beautiful moments in life and to enjoy them in full.

Joy in the Moment

Part of the process of learning to enjoy every moment is to first recognize that there *is* joy in every moment. We must identify an aspect of each endeavor, which appeals to us and to our personal sense of value. Then we can enter into the endeavor passionately and put our full effort into the activity. We may even have to create this sense of value through our actions in order to take joy in the work, particularly when the task itself is not something that we enjoy.

Take the job of cleaning toilets, for example. I was in the California Conservation Corps when I was younger, and we all had to take turns doing bathroom duty (heh, heh) at our dormitory. Nobody liked the job, and I wasn't looking forward to it either. I had never liked cleaning bathrooms. But when my turn came up, I thought to myself, "I'm going to make this bathroom so clean, people are going to talk about it." I wanted to make such an impression, that everyone would come up to me afterwards and say they'd never seen such a clean bathroom (they didn't).

So, I grabbed the mop and bucket and marched into that bathroom with my intentions firmly in mind. I imagined all those nasty little germs and bacteria as my enemy. They must be defeated! I worked diligently, making sure that none escaped, and I took no prisoners.

Afterwards, I realized that it was a job that I could do well, something that I could do passionately, to the best of my ability. I found joy and satisfaction in cleaning those toilets. Not necessarily in the task itself, but rather in how I approached the task.

I find that the eight principles of The Study of True Understanding have allowed me, and many of my students, to find enjoyment and satisfaction in a job that we dislike. For example, we must see the *GROWTH*, if not the *HUMOR* in otherwise unpleasant situations; be *ACCEPTING* of the opportunity we are being given. We must be able to identify and apply our *PASSION* for the job and put all our *STRENGTH* into the endeavor.

In order to be successful in finding joy in the moment, we must also understand and embrace our own mortality. After all, if we're too preoccupied or worried about dying, it becomes very difficult to live in the moment. Conversely, ignoring the fact that we're going to die is no better than is a preoccupation with death. Life is terminal, you know, we just forget to remind ourselves of that fact. We must know and accept that it will happen. We must know that we might die tomorrow, without allowing that knowledge to become an overwhelming paranoiac fear. Then we can get past the fact that we're going to die and accept that we're here to experience. We can only live NOW. The moment is all that we really know that we have.

Some people will recognize their terminal state in life and react by attempting to do everything, to do it ALL now. They scurry around at a frantic pace, filling their lives so full that there is little or no silence, no moments of quiet contemplation available for savoring the experience of life.

The solution to knowing that we have only the moment, is to learn to fully enjoy every moment, not to pack it so full that you're drawn too thin to know or enjoy anything. Spend your life well, but do it moment by moment.

We cannot live effortlessly; we cannot attain complete release without also learning and knowing fear. Because fear rules so much of our lives, we can never know freedom until we are able to recognize and control it.

We must ask ourselves, "Do we fear a situation, or do we simply avoid it?" Knowing to avoid a place or situation isn't necessarily freedom if the reason that we're smart enough to avoid it is because of fear. We need to ask ourselves what our motivations are and learn to recognize when fear is the root.

Fear is not necessarily bad, and should never be ignored. But it must be understood. Fear is an excellent motivator, but it makes a very poor master. Do not let your fears rule you. They are there now, working in indirect, subversive ways to guide and form our actions.

Fear is there to restrict our actions from potentially harmful activity. Fear and pain avoidance, which is simply the fear of pain, are there to keep us safe, healthy and alive. Many fears - fear of embarrassment, fear of ugly hair, fear of being the center of attention, fear of rejection, fear of being alone - serve very little effective purpose, and no fear serves an effective purpose when we allow it to overwhelm us and rule our actions.

Fear is a limitation that cannot be ignored. Further, overcoming our fears requires an acceptance and understanding of the fears and inadequacies of others, as well as our own. We must learn it, know it and accept it in order to gain the control necessary for true freedom and effortless living.

The wisdom of the blind,
is as the blindness of the wise.

The Raw Egg

One evening, after classes had ended, I was sitting on the mat with a small group of students. A student of a local Zen teacher came in and asked if I could assist him. He informed me that he had been given a *Koan* to solve and that he was having difficulty finding an answer. A Koan is a kind of riddle that is used to help a student gain a different perspective on life. He said that he had spoken to a couple of people about his dilemma, and that they had referred him to me.

I asked him specifically, "You want me to give you the answer to this riddle?"

He replied that yes, he needed to have the answer for that night's class, and he hadn't been able to figure it out on his own.

Although I had never met this person before, and was not familiar with his teacher, I agreed to help him. I had him sit down on the mat in front of me and tell me the Koan. When he finished talking, I quickly brought my bamboo stick up and over and struck him on the top of his head.

"OW! What was that for?" he asked.

"That," I told him, "was the answer."

He was obviously puzzled, so I asked him, "Wasn't that the answer you were looking for?" He replied, indignantly, it wasn't.

"Would you like a different answer?" I asked. He said yes, he would. I immediately brought my stick around and slapped him with it on the side of his head.

"OW!" he said again. "Why are you doing that?"

I simply replied that if he was still dissatisfied with my answer I would be happy to give him another. He declined.

"Ah," I said, "you are much closer to finding your own answer already!"

My father was a public school teacher and principal for most of his life. He used to tell me, there's no such thing as a good teacher, there are only good motivators. If you can motivate people to learn, you can teach them anything. I have found this to be absolutely true. It is certainly one of the fundamental concepts in my teaching. Some of the things, martial arts for instance, that I am trying to teach people are very difficult to learn. It is especially difficult for the very young, the five-year-olds who have very little experience in movement, and the thirty-year-olds who are already set in their ways. It is very difficult to learn. They have to be motivated to leave their comfort zone, to be willing to do what's necessary to gain the proper understanding. Then teaching them becomes easy. I'm very rarely frustrated by teaching, because I'm able to motivate my students effectively. That doesn't always mean that I hit them with a stick until they stop asking questions (I reserve that technique for special cases).

When we want to teach people something, we must do it in a way that will make them eager to learn. We need to tailor the exercises, the studies, or the job, to something that they enjoy and to something that they will do cheerfully. If we can make people want to improve their lives, and give them an enjoyable means of acting on that desire, they will change their lives. Remember that the best teachers are really good motivators.

The ancient text of The Art of War states that your subjects must be happy, so that when it comes time to die for you, they will die gladly. It's important to make sure that you're a just and benevolent leader. Then when it comes time to do battle, your troops won't decide that they'd rather have the other guy ruling, and turn to fight against you! Again, this reminds me of how schools and businesses should run.

In our dojo workouts, for instance, it never ceases to amaze me how the students actually push themselves past their normal pain thresholds to complete their exercises. Imagine if our public schools students or your office employees were so motivated. It is important to remember, though, that the motivation is only as effective as the motivator. Along those lines, there must not only be a balance of discipline and enjoyment, but the teacher (boss, parent) must also be willing and able to show through their example that the lessons being taught and the endeavor being pursued, will benefit the practitioner. Ah, this reminds me of yet another story!

Once, a long time ago, there was a king. There were many kings in the country where he lived, but this was the most powerful king. He carried with him, always, a wooden scepter with a hand carved into the top. In the wooden hand there was a raw egg gently cradled.

One day, one of the villagers came to him and asked, "You are such a powerful, wise, and strong king. Why, when all of the other kings have scepters with diamonds and emeralds and great valuable stones on them, do you have a wooden scepter with a carved wooden hand at the top holding an egg?"

And the king replied, "Ruling a kingdom is like holding a raw egg. If you rule with too much force, if you hold the egg too tightly, it will break and be destroyed. But, if you have no rules at all, if you hold that egg too loosely, it will fall from your hand and be destroyed. You must hold an egg just right, so it neither falls nor is crushed, and my scepter is a constant reminder to me of how to rule my kingdom."

This king could have conducted himself as the other kings did, but instead chose to make an example of his rule. He chose to seize the opportunity to demonstrate a better way of living to his people, and he used a very visual aid towards that goal.

One of my students told me this story from her childhood in Korea, a few months after she started training, when I asked her why she chose to train with me. She said that she recognized, in the way the dojo ran, this story from her youth. She saw that I ran my school with just enough discipline that people do what they need to do, for growth; but, with just enough freedom and fun to where people are not upset with doing what they are asked to do. She also saw that, through my example and not just my words, the students wished to follow.

Rich Man, Poor Man

Indulge me for just a moment, as I am sure that this chapter is likely to offend some, if not all. I try to treat everyone equally. I have heard many people speak of the growing chasm between the rich and the poor and, quite frankly, I believe the opposite is occurring. They are becoming more and more alike. Let me give you an example:

John has to spend more money on his car payment than he does on his kids. He spends most of his free time looking for, or doing, drugs. He spends his spare time trying to come up with ways of getting more money for the drug habit he supports. He lies, cheats, and steals his way through his day. He blames the government for taking too much, blames those around him for keeping him from realizing his true potential, and takes none of the blame himself. Is John rich or poor?

Now, before you judge me, let me say that I have been both poor and rich. In fact, I have been middle-class, poor, rich, poor again, and have returned to the middle-class. I have had the opportunity to know people in all phases of their lives as well, and I will tell you that there is very little difference. Oh, one has more money than the other. But, this is a very shallow way of judging an individual's wealth, if you ask me. A better way of looking at the person would be to ask how they have dealt with the adversity in life. How has the individual taken advantage of the opportunities (yes, we all have opportunities) that have presented themselves. How does the person prepare themselves for the next phase of growth or change (again, we all go through change).

When we are born we are like a lump of clay. Some of the lumps are smooth and well shaped. We may be born into wealthy families, or we have loving parents, or we grow up in safe neighborhoods. Others lumps of clay are not so good looking. We may have alcoholic parents, we live amongst crime, and we have little money. But at some time in our lives we start to make choices for ourselves. Very few of us, and I venture none who are reading this book, grow up completely detached from information and outside resources. It is then that we start to shape the lump of clay that we were, into the finished sculpture that we become. This is very much up to us!

I have known people who started out in the worst possible situations and saw to it that they removed themselves from that place and worked themselves into a better place. I have also known people who were given every advantage in life and squandered it into the train-wreck that they became. There is no end to the supply of people and places to which we can turn in order to make our lives into what we want them to be. However, the desire, the motivation, and the work ethic, is something that is sorely lacking. Try this one on for size:

Don't give me excuses as to why you can't. Instead, give me reasons for why you can!

It is far easier to come up with the excuses, and to blame someone or something else for why you are the person you find yourself to be. Well, knock it off! Get help if you need it, in identifying the reasons for your current situation and then take the bull by the horns and make the changes necessary to improve your life. Too many people wait around for the next Power Ball Lottery drawing, or the next government program, or the next relative to die.

The entitlement mentality knows no class boundaries. The rich believe that they should be treated better because they are rich and the poor think that they should be treated better because they are poor. But the truth is that we should all be treated according to what we earn in life. Nobody is owed anything. We should learn to respect others so that we will be respected. We should learn to work hard so that we will be rewarded. We should be taught that the only thing you are born with the right to have, is the *opportunity* for growth and positive change in your life. If you are reading this in the United States, then you have been given that right. It is up to you to do something about it.

When we are young we may feel that our parents owe us something. After all, we did not choose to be born! They decided to have a child and so now they owe us. Well, unfortunately, some people never grow out of that self-serving thought process. Their parents are replaced by government programs, if they are replaced at all, and the buck never stops being passed. Our own failure to grow beyond who we were and how we thought, at seventeen or eighteen years of age, continues on into our mature adult years and is passed on to our children.

Remember, this is about the haves as well as the have-nots! The selfishness that we all witness almost every day of our lives - at work, in traffic, at school, in our homes - is part of a growing mutual thought that the world owes us something rather than an understanding that we owe something to the world. If we are to succeed in making the world a better place to live, we must start right now believing and living the philosophy that *in order to build respect, we have to exercise responsibility.*

The good shepherd plants a seed
and sits patiently watching as the stone grows,
and as a bird, flies off towards the setting sun.

Spit Day

As of this writing, we have just completed a celebration of the First Annual National Spit Day! Well, it wasn't really a national celebration. In fact, it wasn't even a regional one. More like fourteen children and two adults, including myself. Truth be told, there were more expressions of disgust by parents than cards bought when they heard about our Spit Day plans.

But, the reasons behind celebrating Spit Day were profound and I would like to share them with you.

We celebrate all kinds of holidays without any real reason or purpose. We involve our children in these holidays without giving them an explanation beyond some of the ridiculous rituals associated with them. Don't get your short hairs in a knot! Let me give you a couple of examples.

Do you celebrate St. Patrick's Day? Do you wear green, and pinch those who don't? Do you go out and drink green beer until you are so drunk that you will kiss anyone wearing a "kiss me, I'm Irish" button? Do you even know who St. Patrick was? Here, let me clue you in.

St. Patrick was a man who, as a youth, was kidnapped by Irish criminals and sold into slavery in Ireland. He escaped, and later returned to introduce, and convert, the Irish to Christianity.

St. Patrick's Day has nothing to do with snakes, by the way. Nothing to do with leprechauns, which can be wicked little things! It is, or was, a primarily Catholic holiday. It is certainly a cause for celebration among those of the Christian faith, as St. Patrick was instrumental in spreading the faith. But, do you really think that having a designated day of drinking pays respect to the man or the country in which he worked so diligently? Do you really think that children should be taught to pinch other children because they are not wearing green, especially when neither of them knows why they should be wearing green? If I was a kid, and someone randomly came up to me and pinched me, I would probably punch them in the nose!

Let's look at Valentine's Day. It used to be called St. Valentine's Day (another Catholic holiday) before card stores, flower shops, and candy stores decided to commercialize it for the masses. Then we dropped the Saint, I believe, mostly so that we could let school children be sucked into the fray without legal ramifications.

Okay, what is wrong with a day designated to showing those we love that we care for them? Nothing really, other than the fact that most people do not know who St. Valentine was (there were several saints named Valentine).

Most accounts would point to a man who, against the wishes of the emperor, would perform marriages amongst young soldiers. You see, the emperor felt that single soldiers were better than married ones. St. Valentine actually ended up losing his head over this.

By the way, didn't we show those we love how much they mean to us by buying them all kinds of gifts just two months earlier? (Don't even get me started on the number of Jewish children I know, who celebrate Christmas!) Why do we need an excuse to buy flowers or cards for our loved ones, anyway? Don't we show them how much we care on a regular basis? More to the point, do we understand and appreciate who and what we are celebrating?

Holidays were intended to draw our thoughts and attention toward those people or events that have had, or continue to have, a profound effect upon our lives. They are supposed to be days of remembrance and appreciation. They are supposed to be days of reverence. This relates to the previous chapter. It is not necessarily what we celebrate (or what we have and don't have), but rather the misplaced value. The danger of misplaced value is that our children learn to judge the importance of things through our systems of value and, we are beginning to see now, the result of what we have been teaching. Most holidays have become excuses for businesses to close, or worse, to sell us stuff.

Alright, let's get back to Spit Day. Did you know that spit (alright, saliva) plays an important part in your life. In fact, without saliva, we would not be able to hold food in our mouths. Most of it would fall out. Saliva also starts the process of breaking down food for ease of digestion, and it helps the food to travel down our throats, so that we don't choke on it. This is pretty important stuff! Information we should know, and a process we should appreciate. But, the best thing about Spit Day is that it would be difficult for anyone to commercialize. The gross out factor is awesome. We did come up with some great Spit Day games, but I will spare you the details. Needless to say, I do not see this holiday catching on at the public schools!

I hope that the meaning to this chapter has not been lost on you. Celebrate! I love to celebrate. But, be sure that you know what, and why, you are celebrating. Don't do anything just for the sake of doing it, or worse, because a store tells you to buy presents. Spend time discussing with your children the reason for the reverence. Take some time, yourself, to truly appreciate the meaning and the reasons for the celebration. Your holidays will be more fun and your children will be better educated. Oh. and there will be more green beer for me!

True Understanding

No matter how often I tell my students that True Understanding is an experience, and cannot easily be defined, it has become obvious to me that most people need something a bit more tangible in order to get started. Something they can grab onto. I offer this explanation, or definition, of True Understanding under extreme duress as it will surely be misunderstood by most.

True Understanding is the ability to be aware of, and recognize, the opportunities which are offered within every moment of every experience while simultaneously possessing the strength to act upon that awareness. True Understanding is always present and often happens to each of us, without training or preparation, though we may be unaware or too distracted to notice. True Understanding happens in small pieces, a moment here, a moment there. It leads us to a door, which has been closed tightly by our misconceptions of what life should be. Through practice, we are able to break the seal and open the door just a little bit. Once cracked open, it becomes much easier to open this door more and more. Eventually, True Understanding will come to you more often. It builds upon itself over time.

The way you must train, to recognize True Understanding, is through a practice that demands total and complete attention both mentally and physically. You must discipline the mind and body together. For me, martial arts proved to be a valuable tool. It taught me a moving meditation, which forced me to discipline my breathing, my physical movement, and my mental awareness. However, with the current focus on competition and sport application, martial arts may no longer hold the promise for True Understanding that it once did. This is not the case in all training environments, of course, but an individual should be careful when choosing a martial arts school if they are hoping to gain emotional and spiritual strength through their study.

Further, it is important for me to state that while I caution against making value judgments on other people's beliefs, True Understanding must incorporate the eight principles of Acceptance, Concern and Caring, Growth, Strength, Humor, Unconditional Love, Passion, and Vitality. These are principles that are inherent to a life style that will help an individual to be happy, healthy, prosperous, loved and loving.

True Understanding leads us on a path of helping others and service to our community. The words Chi Do Kai translate to "gathered in the study of true understanding." But they can also be interpreted to mean "gathered for the purpose of community service." Interesting, don't you think?

Now, since I am going out on the shaky limb of value judgments, it must be said that I also don't believe that people who inspire negativity in those around them are spiritually evolved, even though they appear to be following their truth, their conviction. Conviction is not True Understanding. Conviction may well be strong enough to appear as True Understanding to most people, but if someone's conviction is harming others it is not True Understanding. There have been many people through history whose convictions led them down negative paths to power and destruction. This has, sadly, been the case in religion as well as politics.

We should remember that many people may understand something well, without possessing True Understanding. Hopefully, all people will decide to look for truth in their lives. But some may decide that the truth in their lives is that they should not have to work, they should not have to respect others. That they should be able to do whatever they feel like doing in the moment, regardless of its impact on others. That's their truth.

I'd say, "Well that's okay" (no value judgments). But that's not True Understanding. They may understand the idea of following their truth, but they don't truly understand the purpose of doing so. Laziness, a lack of respect and immediate self gratification do not lie along a spiritual path. Some people will be inclined, when directed to find and embrace their own truth, to take what seems to be the easiest path. The easy way is to give up on responsibility and pursue immediate gratification. Many people follow their "truths," but this does not mean that they have True Understanding.

So, aside from martial arts, where do we start on a path to True Understanding? How do we find the right teacher or guide? Is this something that takes a lifetime of study to acquire?

Well, there's certainly nothing wrong with spending your entire life reading, studying philosophy and religion, joining churches and other spiritually oriented communities, etc. But our path to True Understanding doesn't need to be that long and convoluted. There's no real need to follow that route.

There's certainly nothing wrong with deciding to take the next twenty years to get to know about your own self through other people's truths. If you read a book on philosophy, you may or may not find a personal truth in that book. If you read five books on philosophy, you will probably find a truth, for you. You'll get teary-eyed and choked up and go, "My God, that's so true!" So you will begin to accumulate a bunch of those truths. At the very least you are creating a solid foundation of personal truths. But, look at all the material you have to go through in order to find those truths. Those truths are also somebody else's idea of what truth is, which means that they are only partially true for you.

For some people, moving around and searching will seem necessary. But, it's a very long way around to finding True Understanding. I'm not saying that you should bypass that route because it's faster to do it yourself. I am saying that it's more effective to walk the path yourself. It's more effective to simply learn to breathe, to think, to act with discipline, and then to go ahead on to the next steps.

It isn't necessarily easier; it's just more effective than taking the roundabout way of looking at forty or fifty different peoples' belief systems and trying to find truth in each of those systems.

Honestly, I ended up taking the roundabout route. I searched, I bounced around. Therefore, I'm not saying it's a bad thing, and it is certainly necessary for some people. But now, at this point in my life, I wonder why anybody would want to go the long way around if it is not needed. I don't believe that you should. But the fact is that it is sometimes easier, and more fun, to ask for company along the way. Just be careful not to fall into the traps that can be laid out by individuals hoping to gain, at your expense, from your journey.

But, what everyone who actually commits that much time to their search will eventually find, is that the answer was within them all the time. It didn't come from any one aspect of what they studied; it came through *all* of what they studied. True Understanding seems too simple, once we find it, but it remains true none-the-less.

But if you are looking for company along the way, how do you know, when you meet a person, that they are the one who can help you develop your spirituality? Well, the impact of the individual's personality or manner upon your first meeting tells a lot. But charisma can be misleading, so you may want to consider the circumstances of your meeting as well. These things may help point out who will be important to you.

When you're searching for a spiritual guide or advisor, you must also be willing to devote a certain amount of time to following his or her path. You must be willing to spend enough time under that person's instruction to understand the lessons. However, if you're carrying around a full cup on your search, the understanding you think you're looking for is going to be very difficult to find. You must be willing to, at least for the moment, empty your thoughts of preconceived notions. Otherwise, you may entirely miss the teacher's point.

Do keep in mind that the more experience you have, the more opinions and knowledge that you have accumulated, the harder it may be to find the teacher that you "expected." You may find yourself disagreeing with everything and everyone simply because you're sure that you already KNOW, even while you can sense that you're still searching.

One candle with flame, a second without.
The first lights the second, the second goes out.

The Man vs. The Message

I know that we have touched upon this subject elsewhere in this book, but the topic deserves a bit more discussion. There have been many times in the history of the world that individuals of truly astounding quality have touched the lives of hundreds and thousands of people. Unfortunately in true human fashion, we attached ourselves to the person rather than to the message, which is what indeed made the individual great in the first place.

Worse, we then build religions around these individuals and begin to revise the message in ways that we deem appropriate for the greater chance of survival of the message itself. Unfortunately, the ego of human beings is such that, when we begin to alter the message of these gifted individuals our own selfishness (unintentionally or not) begins to creep in and make itself known through the obviously skewed interpretations of the very message we devote our lives to preserving! Now, I am not going to name names, after all it is about the message and not about the man, but let's look at an example, and see if you know who I am writing about.

A man comes along and says, "Hey, you know, all this fighting amongst yourselves, especially in the name of God is not only errant, but disrespectful. You're both right in your own way, but wrong in your approach. There is a middle ground. If you all agree on the basic tenets of the faith you follow, stick to those and watch how fruitful and satisfying your lives can be. Come together in your praise, rather than apart, and God will be served!"

Do know who it is? It could be the story of any one of several great thinkers. But, the people he was speaking to, for the most part, were threatened by this message. Their vocation was at stake. Their pride was hurt. Their power would be weakened by such a message, yielding as it was! So, before too much explanation or teaching could occur, the man was put to death.

Now, what do we do with the message? After all, this was a message that could not be denied. Hundreds and hundreds of people had already heard the message and there was an undeniable truth to it! Even after his death, people were flocking to hear the message as delivered by those who had spent only a few years under the tutelage of this man. Truly a great message indeed!

In any case, what we tend to do is build a religion around the man rather than the message. This is important because when someone else teaches the message, especially if that person does not truly understand the message, others will question the validity of the lesson. Herein, the trappings are laid. How do we, as ordinary people, share any message of great importance, without messing it up?

Did you ever play, as a child, the telephone line game? This is the game where one person tells another person a secret, and then that person passes the secret along to another, then that person to another, and so on. Very rarely, if ever, does the last person have the original message correct. In fact, it is usually so messed up that it bares little or no resemblance to the original secret at all! Now imagine that this game is being played by men of power, men with great egos, men who admittedly felt that there may be too great a weakness among ordinary people to live according to a message that was the word of God. Imagine how corrupt the final message would sound!

But this all comes from the ordinary person's attachment to a man versus a message. How often have we heard something from a salesperson that seemed too good to be true, but bought the product or service anyway. Once paid for, when the product or service does not deliver in the way we expected, we say to ourselves (or, even worse, others say to us) that we should have known better. But we believed the person. The salesperson's sincerity, charisma, and appearance helped us to believe in something when we should have known better. Let me shift gears for a moment and offer a personal perspective.

In 1905, a child was born in Khotin, Bessarabia, in Romania. His name was Fischel Cerpok and he was the son of Leib Cerpok. In 1913, Leib Cerpok hid Fischel and his brothers in potato sacks, loaded them onto a wagon, and fled the country. Shortly afterward, in 1919, the village of Khotin was the site of a horrific massacre and the entire town was laid to waste and plowed under. When Fischel and his family arrived in the United States on March 5, 1913, their names were changed and Fischel Cerpok was renamed Philip Rosen.

Coincidentally, I was born on March 5, 1961, a grandson to Philip Rosen. I was named Michael Lewis Rosen (Lewis being the English version of Leib). At the age of nearly 101 years, Philip Rosen (Fischel Cerpok) passed away. Now, while the name Rosen held a great deal of personal history for me, that history was relatively brief, and I wished to honor my heritage by going back to using the name Cerpok. I also wished to pay respect to my great-grandfather, Leib, whom I was named after.

One of the questions that came up repeatedly, while I was making my decision to change my surname was, "What about the following that you have created under the name Michael Rosen? Aren't you afraid of losing the contacts and the credits due to the work you did under that name?" Well, I certainly would not want the credit for something simply because someone who met me once thought I was good enough looking to make sense (I am quite striking, you know) and if the words that I spoke, and the deeds I performed, and the message which I shared as Michael Rosen have any real quality or significance, they will endure. We must not be so eager to think that the impact of our lives is based upon the face or name we associate with a message. If we do, most of us are doomed to obscurity. After all, we do not have the wealth or power to immortalize ourselves in the eyes of others with hospital wings, or libraries, or parks. Now, I am not saying that the philanthropists who donate to the creation of those worthy projects are simply looking for recognition. But rather, that we should all face the fact that our real contribution to our families and our communities lies in how well we lived, loved, and shared a message which brought hope, peace, and quality to life.

Random Ravings

The following are some short thoughts, which I wanted to share. My wife says that all of my thoughts are short (I am only five feet and six inches tall). I choose to believe that I am succinct.

Self Confidence vs Self Esteem

Anyone who looks into martial arts these days will see advertisements espousing the benefits of the martial styles. Chief among these is increased self confidence. But what, really, is the value of self confidence without a simultaneous increase in self esteem?

The martial arts, first and foremost, teach fighting skills. That's why they call it "Martial Arts." But while learning the skill to fight may give students greater confidence, it does not necessarily offer the student a greater understanding of their value to their own selves or to society. A bully on the play ground is confident. The guy who picks a fight in a bar is confident. What leads these people to violent confrontations is more likely a lack in self esteem. The need to prove ourselves to others stems from the need to prove our value to ourselves.

One of the dangers of teaching the martial arts today is that we live in a time of instant gratification. Many schools will promote students to an advanced rank within three years. Plenty of time to instill a measure of self confidence in a student's abilities, but hardly time to make a lasting impact on the true value a student places on their self. Another way to look at this is to ask two simple questions, "Do I feel that I have the ***skill*** to hurt this person?" and, "Do I feel that I have the ***right*** to hurt this person?" The first questions our self confidence, while the second questions our self esteem.

I have had parents of young students express their concern that their child, even after two or three years of training, is still not willing to stand up to the neighborhood bully. I have had some of those same parents come back and tell me how their child, now nineteen years old and after eight years of training, is a confident world traveler who is succeeding in every aspect of his or her life. To be confident in your abilities is fine and good, but to be confident in your value to yourself, your family and your community is what leads to a truly satisfying existence. This is the goal that I have for my students.

The Boob Tube

I read a newspaper article one day about a recent study, which implied that children who watch an hour or more of the television daily are more likely to become violent adults. The article stated further, that it didn't really matter what television shows were being watched.

My jaw dropped! I've ruined my children. I always knew there was something just a little bit fiendish about Big Bird. And have you noticed the teen obsession with vampires? The Count! Yes, it would seem that Sesame Street has once again reared its ugly truth. Remember when we thought that Bert and Ernie were trying to turn our sons into homosexuals?

Now, because the average American watches three to five hours of television a day, it is no wonder that we are such a violent society. Look at your own self? Are you going to sit there and say that you are not raging as you read this? You're not? Oh. Well, to be quite honest, I am not exactly that upset myself. I am certainly not feeling violent. Could it be that maybe, just maybe, violence has more to do with a lack of guidance in our early childhood, than with the amount of television we watch? I mean, I could certainly see where the results of either could be confused. If your five-year-old is watching more than an average amount of television, where are you during that time?

I wonder if anyone has ever bothered to do a study of violent behavior among families who watch television together. I can remember as a child my mother and father and sisters and brothers would all watch television together for an hour, then have a bowl of ice cream and talk about what we had watched. I remember going to the movies with my father and then stopping for pie on the way home and discussing what we had just seen. Granted, we were a well-fed bunch, but as we lived in Chicago, no one seemed to notice. The result of all of this television and movie watching was that none of us turned out to be violent adults.

My point however, is that once again we have managed to find a way to dump the responsibility of how our children turn out, on someone else. We are getting better at it. This time we are not only placing the blame away from ourselves, but we are placing the blame on an inanimate object, that damnable television.

Well, at least the TV can't argue our point! We won't even direct responsibility toward a particular type of television show. Whether we are watching "Leave It To Beaver" reruns or "Buffy, The Vampire Slayer," television is to blame. How ingenious. I remember when studies were blaming the parents and school administrators who imposed corporal punishment for the violence in society. Boy, did they make a stink about being held to blame! No, the old boob tube won't deny responsibility. It won't argue with the result of the study. We have finally figured out a way to truly pass the buck.

But if you happen to be one of those parents who don't really mind raising your child, you may want look in a different direction. A mirror might do well. If you want to know how you sound while driving through heavy traffic, listen to your children as they deal with a frustrating sibling. Want to find out, once and for all, who has been teaching your child those cuss words? Heh, heh. Take a good hard look at how you are dealing with life and the challenges life poses, and I think you will see where the blame should truly fall.

Take responsibility and act as a good example for your children. But don't stop there. When you are looking for activities and ways for your child to stay busy after school or during school breaks when you can not be with them, look for activities which are led by good role models. Try to fill your child's life with positive examples. You know that there will always be negative examples out there for them to see. Don't try to shelter them from all the bad, but rather offset those negative influences with positive ones.

On Faith

Many times I have seen the power of faith. I believe that faith is an important aspect in developing a strong spiritual foundation. Unfortunately, too often blind faith is what is asked for by those leading us down paths that may have been perfectly suited to them, but are totally inappropriate for others.

In fact, I have more often than not witnessed the phrase "have faith" uttered by those who simply did not have good answers. This benefits no one! Blind faith often suggests a lack of inquisitiveness, which leads naturally to a stagnation of growth. Who among us has reached a point of spiritual understanding where growth is no longer needed? Surely none who are still living! In order to grow and continue our experience of True Understanding, we must question.

Find someone who is offended at your questioning of their system of beliefs and you will almost certainly find someone who is still following rather than leading. Not a bad thing, mind you. But if you are putting your "faith" in someone who is still following, why not lead yourself?

Do not misunderstand! We are ALL still learning, all still growing (one would hope). But some are better able to lead individuals toward a personal relationship with God than others. Some will be better suited to guide you towards your own awakening. The teacher must be able to provide some answers to the dilemma of our lives rather than to tell us that we must have faith. Of course, we must have faith. But there is much more to be said!

Lesson one: Shizu kani! In Japanese this means "shut up." Find quiet moments to be at peace with yourself, without the constant drone of our outward existence and incessant muttering of those who would wrap you within their dogma and rhetoric. These are not only religious figures, but personal acquaintances as well. They all have their motives, whether conscious and intentional or not. This includes ME. Take some time to quietly inhale the beauty of the nature which DOES surround all of us.

Act your Rank

I often say "Act your rank, not your belt size." You need to understand that belt sizes for Jujutsu uniforms range from 0 to 8, with 8 being a very large adult. Consequently, an adult may be wearing a belt sized 4, 5 or 6 and these are characteristically temperamental ages. Act your rank, not your belt size.

Particularly at work, it is easy to find people acting their belt size. This may be your supervisor or boss, someone pretty high up, and they throw temper tantrums all the time. Does that behavior encourage your respect of him or her? At a certain point in life you need to begin to act your rank. You're not a child, you know.

And in the End...

We have taught many young children at the ChiDoKai Dojo, and I will occasionally remind my instructors of certain rules that must be followed when working with the children. One of the primary rules is not to assume that the students understand what you are telling them. I explain that teaching martial arts is like teaching a foreign language. Never assume that the student knows what you're talking about. Even the simple things, such as tuck your chin when you roll, step forward...you'd be surprised how many adults, not just the children, get confused when you tell them to step forward.

Many times, when working with children, they will step out with the left foot when you asked for the right, or they put their right arm down when you say left. What does the instructor do? The instructor tells them to switch feet, or switch arms, right? What do you think the student does? They switch arms when you tell them to switch feet. Or, they switch their feet around when you tell them to switch arms.

I have seen instructors do exactly that, and the student is always switching the wrong parts of their body around, and the instructor just continues saying, "Switch this," or, "Switch that..." It's kind of funny to watch, since it might take four or five times before everything is right again. But, it's unnecessary.

I've seen plenty of adults make the same mistake. It isn't that the student really doesn't know the difference between right and left, or between their arms and their legs. But, they're thinking, they're anticipating what you mean, and they get confused.

The point is, in life as in martial arts, don't continue to tell a person what to do when they are obviously confused or don't understand. Step in and show them (touch or move the arm or leg in question), so they'll know exactly what you're talking about. We do not KNOW through words, we KNOW only through doing, through experience.

Everything that's printed is a lie. I often say this during philosophical discussions, and people react quite strongly. However, I do not say it to question the knowledge or intent of any author, but rather to question the awareness and understanding of the reader.

Truth is a matter of perspective. Written words are a reflection of the author's perspective, and will reflect a truth that has been repeatable and verifiable for that individual. Can the reader, however, truly understand that truth from their own, distinctly different perspective? Does the student always understand what the instructor means by "forward" when they are facing each other? (Does she mean her forward, or mine?)

Words are a poor reflection of reality. Words in print become misleading and treacherous because they can be accepted literally as truth. Too many individuals will fail to look beyond what has been placed before them on the printed page, mistakenly substituting rote repetition for thoughtful consideration. We assume that we know because we know the words. But, where is the experience in words?

Experience alone, however, will not necessarily lead us to an understanding of truth. We all need guidance, in one manner or another, to understand and find harmony in our lives. Together, the printed word and personal experience can be effective tools for developing a greater understanding and satisfaction in life. It is my hope that this book has provided a small measure of meaningful guidance.

Your final lesson, accordingly, is to forget the words. Do not trust your understanding of someone else's words; question, experience and gain a True Understanding. This book was a guide, but each lesson goes on much further than what was touched on here. Find and follow your path to an effortless life and your own True Understanding.

An open door, dark as night.

Printed in the United States
55623LVS00004B/46-69

9 781424 138340